The History of the Solomon Islands

Hidden Treasures of the South Pacific

Copyright © 2023 by Nanise Leweniqila and Einar Felix Hansen.

All rights reserved. No part of this publication may be reproduced, stored in a retrieval system, or transmitted, in any form or by any means, electronic, mechanical, photocopying, recording, or otherwise, without the prior written permission of the copyright holder. This book was created with the help of Artificial Intelligence technology.

The contents of this book are intended for entertainment purposes only. While every effort has been made to ensure the accuracy and reliability of the information presented, the author and publisher make no warranties or representations as to the accuracy, completeness, or suitability of the information contained herein. The information presented in this book is not intended as a substitute for professional advice, and readers should consult with qualified professionals in the relevant fields for specific advice.

A Mysterious Archipelago Emerges 6

The Early Indigenous Inhabitants 9

Navigating the Pacific: The Polynesian Connection 12

Melanesian Culture and Traditions 15

Warriors of the Islands: Tribal Conflicts 18

The Arrival of European Explorers 21

Spanish and Portuguese Encounters 24

The British and German Colonial Era 26

World War II in the Solomon Islands 29

The Battle of Guadalcanal 32

Post-War Struggles for Independence 34

The Solomon Islands Gain Sovereignty 37

Modern Challenges and Political Developments 40

Traditional Arts and Crafts 43

Melanesian Music and Dance 46

Indigenous Healing and Belief Systems 49

Flora and Fauna of the Solomon Islands 52

A Gastronomic Journey: Solomon Islands Cuisine 55

Honiara - Capital City and Historical Hub 58

Gizo - Gateway to Western Province 61

Tensions and Triumphs in Auki 64

Exploring the Lush Choiseul Island 67

Ancient Mysteries of Malaita 70

The Serene Beauty of Santa Isabel 73

The Magical Marovo Lagoon 76

Rennell and Bellona: World Heritage Wonders 79

Tikopia - The Island of Sustainability 82

Diving into the Deep: Solomon Islands' Reefs 85

Birdwatching Paradise: Avian Wonders 88

The Solomon Islands' Unique Marine Life 91

Preserving the Past: Museums and Heritage Sites 94

Cultural Festivals and Celebrations 97

Tourism and Sustainable Travel in the Solomon Islands 100

Conclusion 103

A Mysterious Archipelago Emerges

The Solomon Islands, an enigmatic archipelago nestled in the South Pacific Ocean, have long been shrouded in mystery. Spanning over 900 islands, this paradisiacal realm boasts a rich tapestry of history, culture, and natural wonders that beckon explorers and scholars alike. As we delve into the annals of time, the emergence of this mystical archipelago comes to light, revealing a saga that predates recorded history.

Geologically, the Solomon Islands' origins are rooted in the complex interactions of tectonic plates. Situated along the Pacific Ring of Fire, this region is a hotbed of seismic activity, characterized by subduction zones, fault lines, and volcanic eruptions. The islands themselves are remnants of ancient volcanic activity, as well as coral atolls formed over millennia. This geological tumult gave rise to a diverse landscape, from lush rainforests to volcanic peaks and vibrant coral reefs.

The earliest human inhabitants of the Solomon Islands are believed to have arrived around 4,000 years ago, making these islands one of the last places on Earth to be settled by humans. They brought with them a rich maritime culture, renowned for their navigational skills using celestial cues and the ancient art of wayfinding. These intrepid seafarers journeyed across vast stretches of open ocean, connecting the islands with neighboring regions such as Papua New Guinea, Vanuatu, and Fiji. Their voyages were instrumental in shaping the cultural mosaic of the Solomon Islands.

The indigenous peoples of the Solomon Islands, primarily of Melanesian descent, developed distinctive societies with their own languages, customs, and belief systems. These communities thrived in harmony with the bountiful natural resources the archipelago offered. Fishing, agriculture, and the crafting of intricate canoes and tools became integral to their way of life. The ancient cultures of the Solomon Islands were marked by elaborate rituals, oral traditions, and intricate art forms that reflected their deep connection to the land and sea.

Contact with the Western world, however, would irrevocably alter the course of history for the Solomon Islands. Spanish explorer Álvaro de Mendaña was among the first Europeans to arrive in the archipelago in 1568, naming it after the biblical King Solomon. Subsequent European explorers and traders brought with them new influences, including Christianity, firearms, and diseases. The ensuing centuries saw a complex interplay of colonial powers, including the British and Germans, vying for control over these lush, resource-rich islands.

The Solomon Islands played an unwitting role in the theater of World War II, particularly during the pivotal Battle of Guadalcanal. This intense conflict between Allied and Japanese forces left an indelible mark on the islands' history, with remnants of war scattered across the landscape as haunting reminders of that tumultuous period.

In the post-war era, the Solomon Islands embarked on a path toward self-determination, ultimately gaining sovereignty in 1978. Since then, the nation has grappled with political challenges while striving to preserve its unique cultural heritage and natural treasures. The islands have become a crucible of diverse influences, from traditional practices to modern innovations, and continue to evolve in the 21st century.

The Solomon Islands, with their ancient mysteries and vibrant cultures, are a testament to the enduring resilience of their people and the allure of their stunning landscapes. This archipelago, emerging from the depths of geological time and human history, invites us to explore its hidden depths and discover the tales that have shaped its captivating identity.

The Early Indigenous Inhabitants

The early history of the Solomon Islands is intertwined with the presence of its indigenous inhabitants, who settled in this remote archipelago more than four millennia ago. These ancient peoples, often referred to as Melanesians, were the original custodians of this lush and mysterious land.

Archaeological evidence suggests that the first human arrivals in the Solomon Islands can be traced back to around 2000 BCE. These early settlers were intrepid seafarers who embarked on voyages of exploration across the vast expanse of the Pacific Ocean, using outrigger canoes and their deep knowledge of the stars, winds, and ocean currents. Their journeys to these isolated islands are a testament to their exceptional maritime skills and navigational prowess.

Upon their arrival, these early inhabitants found an archipelago of remarkable diversity, both in terms of geography and ecology. The Solomon Islands comprise a vast array of islands, from rugged volcanic peaks to low-lying coral atolls, each offering unique challenges and opportunities for sustenance. Rainforests teemed with an abundance of flora and fauna, providing a rich source of food, medicine, and materials for crafting tools and shelter.

The indigenous peoples of the Solomon Islands developed a complex web of societies, each with its own distinct languages, customs, and traditions. Kinship systems played a central role in their social structures, guiding relationships, obligations, and hierarchies within communities. These early societies were often organized into clans or tribes, each with its own territory and leadership structure.

Spirituality held a profound place in the lives of the early inhabitants. They practiced a rich tapestry of animistic beliefs and ancestral worship, connecting the natural world with the supernatural. Sacred sites, such as stone altars and ancient trees, served as places of reverence and rituals. The indigenous peoples believed that the spirits of their ancestors played a vital role in their daily lives, influencing decisions and offering protection.

The Solomon Islands were not isolated from the broader Pacific cultural exchange. Over centuries, interactions with neighboring island groups, such as Papua New Guinea and Vanuatu, led to the exchange of goods, knowledge, and cultural practices. These interactions contributed to the development of a unique cultural blend that remains a defining aspect of the Solomon Islands today.

Sustenance for these early inhabitants came primarily from their close connection to the land and sea. Fishing, both inshore and deep-sea, provided a consistent source of protein. Agriculture, particularly the cultivation of taro, yam, and sweet potatoes, supplemented their diet. Gathering of edible plants and hunting of wild game further enriched their culinary traditions.

Artistic expression was another hallmark of these early societies. They created intricate pottery, finely woven baskets, and distinctive lapita pottery, marked by intricate patterns and designs. Their oral traditions, passed down through generations, conveyed their history, mythology, and cultural values through storytelling, song, and dance.

As we delve into the annals of time, the early indigenous inhabitants of the Solomon Islands emerge as a resilient and resourceful people, shaped by the challenges and opportunities of their unique environment. Their legacy, deeply rooted in the ancient history of these islands, continues to influence the culture, traditions, and identity of the modern-day Solomon Islands.

Navigating the Pacific: The Polynesian Connection

The history of the Solomon Islands is not one of isolation but rather of interconnectedness with neighboring island groups in the vast expanse of the Pacific Ocean. Among the fascinating connections that have left an indelible mark on the islands' history is the Polynesian influence. The Polynesian connection, although not as pronounced as in other regions of the Pacific, reveals the remarkable navigational skills and cultural exchanges that occurred across these ancient seafaring routes.

Polynesians, who hailed from the region now encompassing modern-day Tonga, Samoa, and Fiji, are celebrated for their extraordinary maritime prowess. Their legendary navigators embarked on journeys that spanned thousands of miles across the Pacific, navigating by the stars, currents, and the flight patterns of migratory birds. This remarkable knowledge allowed them to explore and settle on islands scattered across the Pacific, including the Solomon Islands.

The Polynesian connection to the Solomon Islands is evident in various aspects of culture, language, and even physical artifacts. Linguistic analysis reveals traces of Polynesian words and phrases embedded in some indigenous languages of the Solomon Islands, underscoring the depth of contact and influence between these two distinct cultural groups.

One of the most enduring legacies of the Polynesian connection in the Solomon Islands is the voyaging canoe. These double-hulled canoes were masterpieces of design, allowing Polynesian seafarers to undertake daring and arduous journeys. These canoes were more than just vessels; they were symbols of cultural identity and pride.

The techniques and knowledge of Polynesian navigation, passed down through generations, were adopted and adapted by the indigenous peoples of the Solomon Islands. While the navigational prowess of the Polynesians was awe-inspiring, it was a skill that transcended cultural boundaries. The Solomon Islanders, with their own intricate understanding of the seas, blended their knowledge with Polynesian techniques, resulting in a unique navigation tradition that allowed them to explore and settle the vast archipelago.

The Polynesian influence extended beyond navigation and language. It also left a mark on the agricultural practices of the Solomon Islands. Polynesians brought with them valuable crops such as taro, yam, and breadfruit, which became integral components of the Solomon Islands' diet and culture. The exchange of agricultural knowledge and crops enriched the culinary diversity of the region.

Interactions between Polynesian and Solomon Islander communities were not always harmonious, with tensions and conflicts arising at times over resources and territory. Nevertheless, the enduring legacy of Polynesian navigational techniques and cultural elements is a testament to the lasting impact of these early seafarers on the history and culture of the Solomon Islands.

In the grand tapestry of the Solomon Islands' history, the Polynesian connection is a thread that weaves together the stories of exploration, adaptation, and cultural exchange. It reminds us of the remarkable abilities of these ancient navigators and their enduring influence on the vibrant cultures that call the Solomon Islands home.

Melanesian Culture and Traditions

Melanesia, the vast and diverse region encompassing the Solomon Islands, is a tapestry of cultures, languages, and traditions that have evolved over millennia. At the heart of this intricate mosaic lies the unique and vibrant culture of the indigenous Melanesian peoples of the Solomon Islands.

One of the defining features of Melanesian culture is its diversity. The term "Melanesia" itself, derived from Greek, means "black islands," a reference to the darker skin tones of many of its inhabitants. The Melanesian peoples are not a homogenous group but rather a collection of distinct ethnic groups, each with its own language, customs, and traditions.

Language, in particular, plays a central role in Melanesian identity. The Solomon Islands alone are home to over 70 distinct languages, reflecting the rich linguistic tapestry of the region. These languages belong to various language families, with some sharing similarities due to historical connections, while others are entirely unique.

Art and craftsmanship are integral to Melanesian culture. Across the Solomon Islands, indigenous artists create intricate wood carvings, elaborately woven baskets, and finely detailed pottery. These art forms not only serve as expressions of creativity but also hold cultural and spiritual significance. Traditional carvings often depict ancestral stories and spiritual beings, and they are used in rituals and ceremonies.

Melanesian society is traditionally organized around clans or tribes, with kinship systems shaping social hierarchies and relationships. Within these societies, chiefs or leaders often hold positions of authority, guiding their communities in matters of governance, justice, and decision-making. These leadership roles are typically hereditary, passing from one generation to the next.

Religion in Melanesia is a complex blend of animism, ancestor worship, and spiritual beliefs. The natural world is imbued with spiritual significance, and ancestral spirits are believed to play a vital role in daily life. Sacred sites, such as natural features and ancient trees, are revered, and ceremonies and rituals are conducted to honor and communicate with the spirits.

Traditional Melanesian music and dance are vibrant expressions of culture and identity. Musical instruments such as drums, bamboo pipes, and slit gongs are used to create rhythmic and melodious tunes. Dance, often accompanied by mesmerizing chanting and singing, serves various purposes, from storytelling to celebrating significant life events.

Melanesian cuisine is a reflection of the region's abundance of natural resources. Fish and seafood are staples, sourced from both coastal and inland waters. Root crops such as taro, yams, and sweet potatoes are dietary mainstays, often prepared in diverse ways, including roasting, boiling, and pounding into pastes. Coconut is a ubiquitous ingredient, used in cooking and as a flavor enhancer.

Traditional Melanesian customs and rituals mark key milestones in life, from birth to death. Initiation ceremonies, marriage celebrations, and funeral rites are imbued with cultural significance and are often accompanied by feasting, dance, and song. These events serve not only as social gatherings but also as opportunities to pass down oral traditions and reinforce cultural values.

As we delve into the intricate tapestry of Melanesian culture and traditions, it becomes evident that the indigenous peoples of the Solomon Islands have preserved a rich and diverse heritage that continues to shape their way of life. This vibrant culture is a testament to the resilience, creativity, and deep connection to the land and sea that define the Melanesian identity in this captivating corner of the world.

Warriors of the Islands: Tribal Conflicts

In the annals of Solomon Islands' history, the chapter of tribal conflicts stands as a complex and often turbulent narrative. This region, like many others, has seen the ebb and flow of tribal tensions, which have left a profound impact on its societies and communities.

Tribal conflicts in the Solomon Islands can be traced back to ancient times when the indigenous Melanesian peoples lived in distinct tribal groups, each with its own territory, customs, and leadership structures. These tribes often engaged in rivalries and disputes over resources, land, and prestige, which sometimes escalated into violent confrontations.

One of the primary drivers of tribal conflicts was the concept of land ownership. Land, with its fertile soil and valuable resources, was not only a source of sustenance but also a symbol of tribal identity and status. Disputes over land boundaries, access to fishing grounds, and control of natural resources were common triggers for conflicts.

Traditional warrior cultures emerged within these tribal societies. Warriors were often young men who undertook rites of passage to prove their bravery and readiness to defend their tribes. They trained in combat skills and were well-versed in the use of traditional weapons like spears, clubs, and bows and arrows. The role of warriors extended beyond warfare; they were also tasked with protecting their communities from external threats, including raids by rival tribes.

Conflict resolution mechanisms varied among tribes but often involved negotiations, mediation by respected elders or chiefs, and the payment of compensation, known as "kastom" or "kastom compensation." This system aimed to restore harmony and prevent further bloodshed, reflecting the importance placed on maintaining social order.

While tribal conflicts were a recurrent feature of Solomon Islands' history, they did not define the entirety of the region's social fabric. Many communities coexisted peacefully, engaging in trade, cultural exchanges, and alliances. However, the impact of these conflicts on affected communities was often profound, leading to displacement, loss of life, and economic disruption.

The arrival of European explorers and colonial powers in the 19th and early 20th centuries brought new dynamics to tribal conflicts. The introduction of firearms and other advanced weaponry escalated the scale and intensity of conflicts. Moreover, colonial powers sometimes exploited existing rivalries to maintain control over the indigenous populations.

The aftermath of World War II saw significant changes in the Solomon Islands, as colonial administrations departed and the islands moved toward independence. However, this transition was not without challenges, and the legacy of tribal conflicts continued to affect the nation's progress.

In more recent history, particularly during the late 20th century and early 21st century, the Solomon Islands experienced a period of civil unrest known as the

"Tensions." This conflict, which primarily revolved around political and economic issues, drew upon underlying tribal tensions and had a significant impact on the nation's stability.

Efforts to address tribal conflicts and promote reconciliation have been ongoing, with various peacebuilding initiatives, reconciliation ceremonies, and community-driven programs aimed at healing wounds and fostering unity. These endeavors reflect the resilience and determination of the Solomon Islands' people to move beyond a history marked by tribal conflicts toward a more peaceful and harmonious future.

As we reflect on the complex history of tribal conflicts in the Solomon Islands, we must recognize the enduring spirit of reconciliation and the efforts of communities to build a more peaceful and prosperous nation. This chapter serves as a reminder of the challenges faced and the progress made in navigating the intricate web of tribal dynamics in this remarkable archipelago.

The Arrival of European Explorers

The arrival of European explorers in the Solomon Islands marked a pivotal moment in the history of this remote and enchanting archipelago. It opened a new chapter in the islands' story, one defined by encounters between indigenous cultures and the expanding influence of European powers. These explorers, driven by curiosity, ambition, and the desire to chart the uncharted, ventured into the Pacific, leaving an indelible mark on the Solomon Islands.

The earliest European exploration of the Solomon Islands can be traced back to the late 16th century. In 1568, the Spanish explorer Álvaro de Mendaña de Neyra became one of the first Europeans to set eyes on the islands. He named them "Islas Salomón" after the biblical King Solomon, believing he had discovered the source of the legendary wealth of Solomon.

Mendaña's expedition aimed to establish a colony in the Solomon Islands, but it faced numerous challenges, including disease, resource scarcity, and conflicts with indigenous peoples. After Mendaña's death, the Spanish abandoned their settlement attempts, leaving the islands relatively untouched by European influence for several centuries.

It wasn't until the late 18th century that European explorers returned to the Solomon Islands. British explorers, such as Philip Carteret and John Shortland, made notable voyages to the region in the late 1700s. These explorers charted some of the islands and documented their observations of the indigenous peoples and landscapes.

The 19th century witnessed an influx of European explorers and traders into the Pacific, driven by the desire for resources, scientific discovery, and territorial expansion. The Solomon Islands, with their lush rainforests, fertile soil, and marine riches, became a focal point for these ambitions.

The British, German, and French powers established their presence in the Solomon Islands during this era. In 1886, the British declared a protectorate over the southern Solomon Islands, while the German New Guinea Company claimed the northern islands. These colonial powers sought to exploit the islands' copra (dried coconut kernel) production, which was in high demand for its use in soap and cooking oil.

The interactions between European traders and the indigenous peoples of the Solomon Islands were complex. While trade brought new goods and technologies, it also led to tensions over land, resources, and labor. The introduction of Western diseases, such as measles and influenza, had devastating consequences for the local populations, leading to significant loss of life.

Christian missionaries played a crucial role in the European presence in the Solomon Islands. They arrived in the mid-19th century, aiming to convert the indigenous peoples to Christianity. Over time, Christianity became a dominant influence on the culture and social structures of the islands.

The late 19th and early 20th centuries saw the formal establishment of colonial rule by the British and Germans, which persisted until the aftermath of World War II. During the war, the Solomon Islands became a battleground in the Pacific Theater, particularly during the pivotal Battle of Guadalcanal.

In the post-war era, the Solomon Islands gradually moved toward self-governance and, ultimately, independence. In 1978, the nation gained sovereignty and became a member of the Commonwealth of Nations.

The arrival of European explorers in the Solomon Islands marked a transformative period in the islands' history, characterized by cultural exchanges, conflicts, and the enduring legacy of colonialism. It shaped the trajectory of the nation and its complex relationship with the outside world, setting the stage for the modern Solomon Islands we know today.

Spanish and Portuguese Encounters

The history of the Solomon Islands, a remote and alluring archipelago in the South Pacific, includes intriguing encounters with Spanish and Portuguese explorers during the age of maritime exploration. These encounters, although relatively brief, left an indelible mark on the islands' historical narrative.

The first recorded European contact with the Solomon Islands can be attributed to the Spanish explorer Álvaro de Mendaña de Neyra. In 1568, Mendaña embarked on a voyage across the Pacific Ocean, fueled by the allure of discovering new lands and potential riches. His expedition led him to the Solomon Islands, and he promptly named them "Islas Salomón" after the biblical King Solomon.

Mendaña's journey was an adventurous undertaking, fraught with challenges and hardships. His fleet consisted of two ships, the Santa Isabel and the San Felipe, and carried a mix of Spanish colonists, soldiers, and missionaries. They hoped to establish a colony on the islands and exploit the perceived wealth of the region.

Upon their arrival in the Solomon Islands, the Spanish expedition encountered indigenous peoples who had inhabited the islands for millennia. These indigenous Melanesian communities had developed complex societies, each with its own language, culture, and traditions. The arrival of the Europeans marked a significant and disruptive moment in their history.

Mendaña's expedition aimed to establish a settlement named "Nueva Castilla" on the island of Santa Isabel. However, their venture was fraught with challenges. The Spanish settlers faced difficulties in adapting to the unfamiliar environment and struggled with issues such as disease, resource scarcity, and conflicts with the indigenous peoples.

Ultimately, Mendaña's colony proved unsustainable, and he died during the expedition. Following his death, the Spanish abandoned their settlement attempts in the Solomon Islands, leaving the islands relatively untouched by European influence for several centuries.

The Portuguese also had brief encounters with the Solomon Islands during their maritime explorations in the 16th century. Portuguese explorer Álvaro de Mendonça may have reached parts of the Solomon Islands during his voyages in the early 16th century, although detailed records of his travels are scarce.

The Portuguese and Spanish encounters with the Solomon Islands were early chapters in the islands' interactions with the wider world. While these explorers did not establish lasting European presence or influence in the region, their voyages added to the evolving knowledge of the Pacific and its diverse cultures.

In the centuries that followed, other European powers, such as the British and the Germans, would establish their presence in the Solomon Islands, leading to more enduring interactions and complex colonial legacies. Nonetheless, the brief encounters of Spanish and Portuguese explorers in the 16th century serve as important milestones in the early history of these captivating islands in the South Pacific.

The British and German Colonial Era

The colonial era in the Solomon Islands, characterized by the presence of British and German powers, is a chapter in the archipelago's history that brought significant change and challenges to its indigenous peoples.

The British presence in the Solomon Islands began in the late 19th century. In 1886, the United Kingdom declared a protectorate over the southern Solomon Islands, marking the formal start of British colonial rule. This move aimed to secure British interests in the region, particularly the valuable copra industry, which was in high demand for its use in soap and cooking oil.

During the colonial period, the British established administrative structures and introduced Western-style governance. They appointed resident commissioners to oversee the administration of the protectorate. The imposition of Western legal systems and British law fundamentally changed the way justice was administered in the Solomon Islands, replacing traditional customs and practices.

Christian missionaries played a significant role in the British colonial era, as they sought to convert the indigenous population to Christianity. These missionaries established schools, churches, and medical facilities across the islands, contributing to the spread of Christianity and the transformation of local cultures.

While the British established their presence in the southern Solomon Islands, the northern islands fell under the control of the German New Guinea Company in the late 19th century. Germany, like the British, sought to exploit the islands' copra resources. This division of colonial influence resulted in the northern Solomon Islands coming under German administration, while the southern islands remained under British control.

The German administration introduced economic and agricultural changes to the northern islands, encouraging the cultivation of copra, cocoa, and other cash crops. These efforts significantly impacted the local economies and lifestyles of the indigenous peoples.

World War I brought a temporary halt to the British and German colonial presence in the Solomon Islands. In 1914, Australian forces occupied the German-administered northern islands, effectively ending German colonial rule in the region. The British colonial administration continued in the southern islands.

Following World War I, the League of Nations awarded the mandate for the German-administered northern islands to Australia. This mandate led to a reconfiguration of colonial boundaries in the Solomon Islands.

The British and Australian administrations during the colonial era were not without challenges. Indigenous populations faced the impact of introduced diseases, changes in land ownership, and disruptions to traditional ways of life. Land alienation and labor practices, such as indentured labor, were contentious issues during this period.

The Solomon Islands became a battleground during World War II, particularly during the Battle of Guadalcanal. This conflict between Allied and Japanese forces left a lasting mark on the islands and further disrupted colonial rule.

In the post-war era, the Solomon Islands gradually moved toward self-governance and, ultimately, independence. The legacy of the British and German colonial era left a complex imprint on the islands, shaping the nation's history, culture, and political landscape.

The colonial era in the Solomon Islands was a transformative period marked by the presence of British and German powers, the introduction of Western governance, and the enduring impact of Christian missions. It was a time of profound change and adaptation for the indigenous peoples, laying the foundation for the modern nation that would emerge in the 20th century.

World War II in the Solomon Islands

World War II cast its long shadow over the Solomon Islands, transforming this remote Pacific archipelago into a pivotal theater of conflict. The war's impact on the islands, particularly the Battle of Guadalcanal, left an enduring mark on their history and played a crucial role in shaping the nation that would emerge in the post-war era.

The Solomon Islands, strategically located in the South Pacific, became a focal point for both Allied and Japanese forces during World War II. The Japanese sought to expand their Pacific empire, and the Allies, determined to halt their advance, recognized the islands' significance.

The Battle of Guadalcanal, which began on August 7, 1942, marked a turning point in the Pacific Theater. It was the first major offensive by Allied forces against the Japanese in the Pacific, and it unfolded on and around the island of Guadalcanal in the southern Solomon Islands.

Guadalcanal quickly became a battleground, with fierce fighting taking place on land, in the air, and at sea. The struggle for control of the island involved a series of grueling and often brutal engagements, earning it the nickname "the Island of Death."

The airfield on Guadalcanal, known as Henderson Field, was a critical prize. Both sides recognized its strategic importance, as control of the airfield meant dominance over the airspace and the ability to resupply and reinforce troops on the ground.

The Battle of Guadalcanal was characterized by intense and protracted combat. The U.S. Marines and other Allied forces engaged in relentless jungle warfare against well-entrenched Japanese defenders. The conditions were harsh, with disease, harsh terrain, and heavy rain adding to the challenges faced by both sides.

The naval battles around Guadalcanal were equally intense. The seas surrounding the Solomon Islands became the scene of fierce engagements, as the U.S. Navy and Japanese Imperial Navy clashed in a series of pitched battles. The naval battles of Savo Island, Eastern Solomons, and Santa Cruz Islands were pivotal moments in the campaign.

The Battle of Guadalcanal was not only about military strategy but also about logistics. Supply lines, or the lack thereof, played a decisive role in the outcome of the conflict. Both sides struggled to maintain their troops and equipment in the face of logistical challenges.

The battle ended in early 1943 when the Japanese evacuated the island, marking a significant Allied victory. The cost of the battle was high, with substantial casualties on both sides, but it was a turning point in the Pacific War.

World War II had a profound impact on the Solomon Islands. The conflict brought destruction and disruption, with villages, infrastructure, and landscapes scarred by the ravages of war. Indigenous populations faced hardships and upheaval as they were caught in the crossfire.

After the war, the Solomon Islands experienced a period of post-war reconstruction and recovery. The legacy of World War II, however, endures in the form of war relics, sunken ships, and historical sites that serve as reminders of the conflict's enduring impact on the islands.

World War II in the Solomon Islands is a chapter of sacrifice, resilience, and transformation. It is a testament to the courage of those who fought, the endurance of those who lived through it, and the enduring legacy it left on the nation's history and identity.

The Battle of Guadalcanal

The Battle of Guadalcanal, a pivotal and protracted conflict in the Pacific Theater of World War II, etched its place in history as one of the most grueling and strategically significant battles of the entire war. It unfolded on the island of Guadalcanal, located in the southern Solomon Islands, and it represented the first major Allied offensive against the Japanese in the Pacific.

The battle commenced on August 7, 1942, when U.S. Marines, along with other Allied forces, landed on the shores of Guadalcanal. Their primary objective was to secure an airfield on the island, known as Henderson Field, which held immense strategic importance. Henderson Field, once captured, could be used to launch air operations and support naval activities in the region.

The initial stages of the Battle of Guadalcanal saw intense fighting as U.S. Marines clashed with well-entrenched Japanese defenders. The dense jungle terrain, oppressive heat, and torrential rain made the battle a grueling test of endurance for both sides. Battles like the fight for Bloody Ridge and Edson's Ridge would become legendary for their ferocity.

As the battle raged on, control of Henderson Field shifted back and forth between the Allies and the Japanese. This airfield became a focal point of the conflict, as its possession allowed the controlling side to dominate the skies and resupply and reinforce their ground forces.

The naval battles surrounding Guadalcanal were equally fierce. The seas around the Solomon Islands witnessed a series of intense engagements between the U.S. Navy and the

Japanese Imperial Navy. The Battle of Savo Island, the Battle of the Eastern Solomons, and the Battle of the Santa Cruz Islands were among the pivotal naval confrontations during the campaign.

Supply and logistics were major challenges for both sides. The isolation of Guadalcanal made it difficult to maintain troops and equipment, leading to what became known as the "Cactus Air Force," an amalgamation of U.S. Marine and Navy aircraft that operated from Henderson Field. The Japanese, too, struggled to sustain their forces, facing logistical hurdles and losses at sea.

The Battle of Guadalcanal was not solely a military campaign; it was a test of endurance and survival. Both the Allied and Japanese troops endured brutal conditions, from constant combat and air raids to the harsh tropical environment and rampant diseases like malaria. The physical and psychological toll on the soldiers was immense.

The conflict culminated in early 1943 when the Japanese evacuated Guadalcanal, marking a significant victory for the Allies. The battle's outcome was hard-won, with substantial casualties on both sides, but it was a turning point in the Pacific War. Guadalcanal became a symbol of American resolve and marked the beginning of a broader Allied offensive against Japan in the Pacific.

The legacy of the Battle of Guadalcanal endures in history and in the physical landscape of the Solomon Islands. War relics, sunken ships, and historical sites serve as tangible reminders of the sacrifices made during this arduous campaign. The battle's impact on the Solomon Islands and its role in shaping the nation's history and identity is immeasurable.

Post-War Struggles for Independence

The aftermath of World War II ushered in a period of significant change and transition for the Solomon Islands. The nation emerged from the conflict deeply impacted by the war's ravages, but it also carried with it the seeds of aspirations for self-determination and independence.

As the war drew to a close, the Solomon Islands, like many other parts of the Pacific, faced the challenge of post-war reconstruction. The conflict had left indelible scars on the islands, with villages, infrastructure, and landscapes bearing the physical and emotional marks of war.

In the wake of World War II, the Solomon Islands found themselves under the administration of Allied forces. Australia, in particular, played a prominent role in shaping the post-war trajectory of the nation. The Australian government was entrusted with the governance of the Solomon Islands as part of the broader post-war responsibilities.

While the immediate priority was to rebuild and rehabilitate the islands, the post-war period also saw the emergence of nascent political movements advocating for greater self-determination and autonomy. Indigenous leaders and activists began to voice their aspirations for a future where the people of the Solomon Islands could govern themselves.

The journey towards self-determination was not without challenges. The legacy of colonialism, with its impact on land ownership, governance structures, and economic systems, posed complex issues that needed to be addressed. Indigenous populations sought to regain control over their land and resources, asserting their rights and sovereignty.

Educational institutions played a vital role in nurturing a sense of national identity and political consciousness. Schools and universities in the Solomon Islands became spaces where young leaders and intellectuals began to engage in discussions about the nation's future. The exchange of ideas and the dissemination of knowledge were catalysts for political awareness.

Efforts to achieve greater autonomy culminated in the establishment of the Solomon Islands Council of Chiefs in 1952. This council, representing various indigenous communities, sought to provide a unified voice for the nation's aspirations and concerns. The council's formation marked a significant step towards indigenous self-governance.

Throughout the 1950s and 1960s, the movement for self-determination gained momentum. Indigenous leaders, such as Peter Kenilorea and Solomon Mamaloni, emerged as influential figures in the struggle for independence. They engaged in dialogues with colonial authorities, advocating for increased political representation and the gradual transition to self-rule.

In 1976, the Solomon Islands achieved a significant milestone on the path to independence with the establishment of a new constitution. This constitution laid the groundwork for a parliamentary system of government and granted greater autonomy to the nation. On July 7, 1978, the Solomon Islands officially gained independence from colonial rule.

Independence brought both opportunities and challenges. The nation faced the task of building its institutions, economy, and governance structures. The legacy of colonialism continued to influence the nation's development, as leaders sought to balance the preservation of cultural traditions with the demands of modernization.

The post-war struggles for independence marked a transformative period in the Solomon Islands' history. The nation emerged from the shadows of colonialism as a sovereign state, defined by its rich cultural heritage and the resilience of its people. The challenges of the post-war era would shape the trajectory of the modern Solomon Islands, as it embarked on a path of self-determination and nation-building.

The Solomon Islands Gain Sovereignty

The journey of the Solomon Islands toward sovereignty and independence culminated in a historic moment that forever changed the nation's course. The attainment of sovereignty marked the end of colonial rule and the beginning of a new era defined by self-governance and the aspirations of its people.

On July 7, 1978, the Solomon Islands officially gained independence from colonial rule. This momentous occasion marked the culmination of decades of struggle, advocacy, and negotiation between indigenous leaders and colonial authorities.

The road to independence was not without challenges. The legacy of colonialism had left a complex web of social, economic, and political dynamics that needed to be addressed. Indigenous leaders, such as Peter Kenilorea and Solomon Mamaloni, played pivotal roles in navigating these complexities and guiding the nation toward self-determination.

The establishment of a new constitution in 1976 laid the foundation for the nation's governance structure. Under this constitution, the Solomon Islands adopted a parliamentary system of government, with a Prime Minister and a system of representation that reflected the diverse communities and regions of the country.

Independence also brought with it the responsibility of building and maintaining institutions that would support the nation's sovereignty. The Solomon Islands had to establish government ministries, develop legal frameworks, and create mechanisms for decision-making and governance.

One of the immediate challenges faced by the newly independent nation was economic development. The Solomon Islands' economy was heavily reliant on agriculture, fisheries, and forestry, and efforts were made to diversify and modernize these sectors. The nation also looked to international partners for support in infrastructure development and capacity building.

The preservation of cultural traditions and the protection of natural resources were central to the nation's identity and future. Indigenous customs and practices continued to be valued and respected, while efforts were made to strike a balance between modernization and cultural heritage.

As the Solomon Islands gained sovereignty, it also assumed a place on the global stage. The nation became a member of the United Nations and established diplomatic relations with countries around the world. This newfound international presence allowed the Solomon Islands to engage in global forums and advocate for its interests on a broader scale.

The challenges faced by the newly independent nation were not limited to the domestic sphere. The Solomon Islands' strategic location in the Pacific brought regional and geopolitical considerations into play. The nation became part of regional organizations and alliances, contributing to discussions on security, economic cooperation, and environmental protection in the Pacific region.

The journey toward sovereignty was a testament to the resilience and determination of the Solomon Islands' people. It represented the realization of a dream held by generations of indigenous leaders and citizens who had worked tirelessly to shape their own destiny.

The attainment of sovereignty marked a new chapter in the history of the Solomon Islands, one defined by self-governance, nation-building, and the aspirations of a people who had come together to shape their future. As the nation looked ahead, it carried with it the lessons of its past and the promise of a brighter tomorrow.

Modern Challenges and Political Developments

The modern history of the Solomon Islands is a complex tapestry of challenges, political developments, and societal changes. Since gaining independence in 1978, the nation has navigated a path marked by progress and setbacks, striving to address pressing issues while advancing its aspirations.

One of the prominent challenges faced by the Solomon Islands in the modern era has been maintaining political stability. The nation's political landscape has seen periods of turbulence, marked by changes in leadership, no-confidence motions, and political rivalries. These dynamics have at times posed obstacles to effective governance and development.

Ethnic tensions and regional divisions have also played a role in shaping the nation's political landscape. The Solomon Islands experienced a period of civil unrest and ethnic conflict known as the "Tensions" during the late 1990s and early 2000s. This conflict, rooted in political and economic grievances, had significant social and economic repercussions.

Efforts to address these challenges and promote reconciliation and peace have been ongoing. Various peacebuilding initiatives, reconciliation ceremonies, and community-driven programs have sought to heal wounds and foster unity among the nation's diverse communities.

The Solomon Islands' economy has also faced modern challenges. While agriculture, fisheries, and forestry remain vital sectors, the nation has sought to diversify and modernize its economy. Tourism, for example, has emerged as a significant industry, attracting visitors with its natural beauty and cultural heritage.

Environmental conservation has become a critical concern, as the Solomon Islands grapples with the effects of climate change and the need to protect its unique ecosystems. Rising sea levels, coral bleaching, and extreme weather events pose significant threats to the nation's natural resources and coastal communities.

Healthcare and education have seen improvements in accessibility and quality, with efforts to expand healthcare services and enhance educational opportunities. The Solomon Islands has also sought international partnerships and support for capacity-building in various sectors.

In the realm of governance, the nation has made efforts to strengthen democratic institutions and processes. Elections have been held regularly, allowing citizens to exercise their democratic rights. The country's political leaders have engaged in dialogue and negotiation to address pressing issues and advance national interests.

The Solomon Islands' foreign policy has focused on maintaining diplomatic relations with countries around the world and participating in regional organizations and alliances. The nation has sought to contribute to discussions on regional security, economic cooperation, and environmental protection in the Pacific region.

Challenges such as corruption, infrastructure development, and healthcare access persist, and addressing them remains a priority for the nation's leaders and citizens. The Solomon Islands continues to work toward achieving sustainable development goals and improving the well-being of its people.

The story of the Solomon Islands in the modern era is one of resilience, adaptation, and aspiration. As the nation faces contemporary challenges and navigates political developments, it draws upon its rich cultural heritage and the determination of its people to shape a brighter future. The path ahead holds both opportunities and complexities, as the Solomon Islands continues to define its place in the global community while preserving its unique identity.

Traditional Arts and Crafts

The Solomon Islands, with its rich cultural heritage and diverse indigenous communities, boasts a vibrant tradition of arts and crafts that reflects the creativity, skills, and deep-rooted cultural significance of these practices.

One of the most iconic forms of traditional art in the Solomon Islands is woodcarving. The skilled artisans of the islands have been carving intricate designs into various types of wood for generations. These carvings often depict mythological figures, animals, and ancestral spirits, and they are used for both decorative and functional purposes. Intricately carved canoe prows, war clubs, and house posts are among the most notable examples of Solomon Islands woodcarving.

Bark cloth, known locally as "tapa," is another important traditional craft. Tapa is made from the inner bark of certain trees, which is pounded, stretched, and decorated with intricate patterns. The process of making tapa is labor-intensive and requires a high level of skill. Tapa is used for clothing, ceremonial purposes, and as decorative art. The designs on tapa often carry cultural and symbolic meanings.

Shell money, locally known as "shell currency" or "shell money rings," is a traditional form of currency and ornamentation. These small, circular disks are painstakingly crafted from various types of shells and then strung together to create necklaces or belts. Shell money has deep cultural significance and is often used in ceremonies and exchanges between communities.

Traditional pottery in the Solomon Islands is another ancient craft that has been practiced for centuries. Local potters use clay from riverbanks and volcanic ash to create a wide range of pottery items, including cooking pots, water containers, and ceremonial vessels. The pottery is often adorned with intricate designs and motifs, adding an artistic element to its functionality.

Basketry is another traditional craft that plays a practical role in daily life. Skilled weavers create baskets and containers from locally sourced materials, such as coconut palm leaves, pandanus, and bamboo. These baskets are used for storage, carrying goods, and even as fishing traps. The art of basket weaving is passed down through generations, and each region has its distinctive weaving styles and techniques.

Traditional dance and music are integral to the cultural fabric of the Solomon Islands. Dance performances often feature elaborate costumes, body painting, and rhythmic movements that tell stories, convey legends, and celebrate community events. Musical instruments, including panpipes, bamboo flutes, and drums, accompany these performances, creating a rich auditory experience.

The art of storytelling is deeply ingrained in Solomon Islands culture. Oral traditions have been passed down through generations, preserving history, legends, and moral lessons. Storytelling is often accompanied by music, dance, and visual elements, creating a multisensory experience that engages both young and old.

In recent years, efforts have been made to preserve and promote traditional arts and crafts in the Solomon Islands. Local artisans and cultural organizations have worked to ensure that these ancient practices continue to thrive and evolve. Traditional art forms are celebrated at cultural festivals and events, where they serve as a means of connecting the past with the present and fostering a sense of identity and pride among the Solomon Islands' diverse communities.

The traditional arts and crafts of the Solomon Islands are a testament to the creativity and cultural richness of its people. These practices have not only shaped the material culture of the islands but also serve as a living link to the past, connecting generations and communities through shared traditions, stories, and artistic expressions.

Melanesian Music and Dance

Melanesian music and dance are vibrant expressions of culture, tradition, and identity in the Solomon Islands. The archipelago's diverse communities have cultivated a rich tapestry of musical and dance forms, each carrying its unique history, meaning, and significance.

Music is an integral part of everyday life in the Solomon Islands. It permeates communal gatherings, rituals, celebrations, and ceremonies. Traditional Melanesian music is characterized by a melodic complexity that reflects the intricate rhythms of nature and life on the islands.

One of the most iconic instruments in Solomon Islands music is the panpipe, locally known as "tambu." These instruments are crafted from bamboo and are used in various types of performances, from sacred rituals to festive celebrations. Panpipe ensembles produce melodious tunes that resonate with the soul of the islands.

Drumming is another fundamental component of Melanesian music. Traditional drums, often made from hollowed-out tree trunks or logs covered with animal skins, are used to create rhythmic patterns that accompany dances. The beat of the drum is the heartbeat of many Solomon Islands communities, signaling communal activities and events.

Stringed instruments, such as the guitar and ukulele, have also found their place in Melanesian music. These instruments, introduced by European explorers and missionaries, have been incorporated into local musical traditions, creating a fusion of styles that is both unique and harmonious.

Vocal music is at the heart of Solomon Islands' cultural expression. Singing is a central component of religious ceremonies, storytelling, and social gatherings. Harmonious choral singing is a cherished tradition, with communities often forming choirs that enchant audiences with their melodious voices.

Dance is inseparable from music in Melanesian culture. Traditional dance performances are characterized by intricate movements, expressive gestures, and colorful costumes. Each dance tells a story, conveying legends, myths, and historical events. Dancers use their bodies to paint pictures, acting as living vessels of cultural memory.

The "Tautoga" dance, for instance, is a warrior dance that showcases strength, agility, and bravery. Dancers adorned with traditional ornaments and war paint enact battle scenes, preserving the warrior spirit of their ancestors. Another famous dance is the "Lakalaka," a celebratory dance performed during festive occasions, weddings, and ceremonies, where intricate choreography and harmonious singing are central.

The "Malaita Eagle Dance," also known as the "Saka Saka" dance, is a striking example of the Solomon Islands' diverse dance forms. Dancers wear costumes resembling eagles and perform a dance that mimics the majestic flight of these birds. The "Kastom" dance, on the other hand, is deeply rooted in indigenous traditions and serves as a means of connecting with ancestral spirits.

Modern influences have also made their mark on Melanesian music and dance. Contemporary genres, such as reggae and hip-hop, have found popularity among the youth, blending with traditional rhythms to create new forms of expression. These modern styles often convey messages of identity, social change, and empowerment.

Cultural festivals and events provide platforms for showcasing the rich tapestry of Melanesian music and dance. Festivals like the "Festival of Pacific Arts" offer opportunities for communities to come together, exchange cultural practices, and celebrate their heritage on an international stage.

Melanesian music and dance are not static forms but living traditions that evolve and adapt while remaining deeply rooted in cultural heritage. They serve as a powerful means of preserving the identity, stories, and values of the Solomon Islands, connecting past generations with those of the present and future. In their harmonious rhythms and graceful movements, Melanesian music and dance capture the essence and spirit of these enchanting islands in the South Pacific.

Indigenous Healing and Belief Systems

Indigenous healing and belief systems in the Solomon Islands are deeply intertwined with the spiritual, cultural, and natural aspects of life. These traditional practices have been passed down through generations and continue to play a vital role in the health and well-being of the islands' communities.

Central to indigenous healing in the Solomon Islands is the belief in a holistic approach to health, where the physical, spiritual, and emotional aspects of an individual are interconnected. Traditional healers, often known as "kastom doctors" or "kastom healers," serve as intermediaries between the human world and the spirit world.

One of the core principles of indigenous healing is the belief in the power of ancestral spirits. These spirits are seen as protectors, guides, and sources of wisdom. Healers often seek to establish a connection with these spirits through rituals, ceremonies, and offerings. The spirits are believed to provide guidance, healing energy, and protection to individuals and communities.

Herbal medicine is a fundamental aspect of traditional healing practices in the Solomon Islands. Indigenous healers have an extensive knowledge of local plants, herbs, and natural remedies. They use these resources to treat a wide range of ailments, from physical injuries to spiritual imbalances. Herbal medicine is often administered in the form of teas, poultices, or ointments.

Another integral component of indigenous healing is massage and bodywork. Healers use their hands, often incorporating oils or balms, to manipulate and soothe the body. These techniques are believed to release tension, promote circulation, and restore balance to the body's energies.

Traditional ceremonies and rituals are essential for healing and spiritual cleansing. These rituals may involve chanting, singing, dancing, and the use of sacred objects. Ceremonies are conducted in accordance with specific cultural and spiritual traditions, and they are intended to invoke the aid of ancestral spirits in the healing process.

Dream interpretation is another significant aspect of indigenous belief systems in the Solomon Islands. Dreams are seen as messages from the spirit world and are often consulted for guidance and insight. Healers, known as "dream interpreters," help individuals understand the meaning of their dreams and how they relate to their physical and emotional well-being.

The concept of "taboo" or "kastom law" is also deeply embedded in indigenous belief systems. Taboos are cultural and spiritual restrictions that govern behavior and interactions within communities. Violating taboos is believed to bring about spiritual consequences and illness. Traditional healers often play a role in addressing the consequences of taboo violations and helping individuals seek forgiveness and healing.

In cases of illness or misfortune, individuals may seek the guidance of a traditional healer before turning to Western medicine. The holistic approach of indigenous healing recognizes the interconnectedness of physical, emotional, and spiritual well-being. While Western medicine has become more accessible in the Solomon Islands, traditional healing practices continue to hold a significant place in the hearts and minds of the people.

It is essential to note that indigenous healing and belief systems are diverse across different regions of the Solomon Islands. Each community may have its unique practices, rituals, and healers. While these practices are deeply rooted in tradition, they also adapt and evolve in response to changing circumstances and influences.

In conclusion, indigenous healing and belief systems in the Solomon Islands are an integral part of the nation's cultural fabric. They reflect a deep connection to the land, ancestral spirits, and the wisdom passed down through generations. These practices continue to provide comfort, guidance, and healing to the people of the Solomon Islands, enriching their lives and reinforcing their cultural identity.

Flora and Fauna of the Solomon Islands

The Solomon Islands, nestled in the heart of the South Pacific, are a biological treasure trove teeming with diverse flora and fauna. Its lush rainforests, pristine coral reefs, and unique ecosystems have earned it a place among the world's biodiversity hotspots.

Starting with the flora, the islands are home to an astonishing array of plant species. Towering trees, dense canopies, and a profusion of understory vegetation characterize the rainforests that cover a significant portion of the archipelago. Among the most iconic trees are the Solomon mahogany and the towering kauri pine, known for their valuable timber. Many of these trees are endemic, meaning they are found nowhere else in the world.

The Solomon Islands are renowned for their vibrant and diverse orchid species. These exquisite flowers, with their myriad shapes, sizes, and colors, can be found throughout the islands, adorning trees, rocks, and forest floors. Orchid enthusiasts flock to the Solomon Islands to witness the astonishing variety of these tropical blooms.

Carnivorous pitcher plants, some of which are endemic to the islands, are another botanical marvel. These plants, known as Nepenthes, have modified leaves that form pitfall traps to capture insects. The Solomon Islands are a hotspot for Nepenthes diversity, with numerous species and hybrids discovered in its forests.

Fruit-bearing trees and plants are abundant, providing sustenance for both wildlife and local communities. Coconut palms, breadfruit trees, and various species of bananas are staples of the Solomon Islands' diet. The islands also boast an impressive array of nut trees, including the distinctive betel nut.

The Solomon Islands' rich biodiversity extends to its fauna, making it a haven for wildlife enthusiasts and conservationists. The avian diversity here is exceptional, with numerous endemic bird species. The Solomon Islands sea eagle, the Solomons cockatoo, and the critically endangered Guadalcanal moustached kingfisher are just a few of the unique avian inhabitants.

Reptiles and amphibians are also well-represented in the archipelago. The Solomon Islands are home to a variety of geckos, skinks, and snakes, some of which are found nowhere else on Earth. The islands are particularly famous for the prehistoric-looking crocodile skink, an odd reptile with a distinctive, armored appearance.

Marine life in the Solomon Islands is equally captivating. The coral reefs that fringe the islands' coastlines are among the most biodiverse on the planet. These reefs are teeming with colorful coral formations, anemones, and an astonishing variety of fish species. Divers and snorkelers are treated to a world of vibrant marine life, including parrotfish, clownfish, and reef sharks.

The Solomon Islands are also a significant nesting ground for sea turtles, including the hawksbill and the critically endangered leatherback. These graceful creatures return to the islands' beaches to lay their eggs, a mesmerizing sight for those fortunate enough to witness it.

In the surrounding waters, the islands are visited by magnificent marine megafauna. Spinner dolphins, orcas, and various species of whales, including the humpback and the pygmy killer whale, are known to frequent these seas.

The terrestrial wildlife of the Solomon Islands includes several mammal species, though many are nocturnal and elusive. Bats are among the few native mammals, with the flying fox being the most recognizable. Introduced mammals such as rats and pigs have had a significant impact on the islands' ecosystems.

Conservation efforts are ongoing to protect the unique flora and fauna of the Solomon Islands. National parks and marine reserves have been established to safeguard critical habitats and promote sustainable practices. Indigenous communities are actively involved in conservation initiatives, recognizing the intrinsic value of their natural heritage.

In conclusion, the Solomon Islands' flora and fauna constitute a remarkable tapestry of biodiversity. Its ecosystems, from lush rainforests to vibrant coral reefs, are a testament to the importance of preserving these natural wonders for future generations. The islands stand as a living testament to the intricate interplay between human culture and the environment, where indigenous knowledge and traditions continue to nurture and protect the magnificent flora and fauna that call this paradise home.

A Gastronomic Journey: Solomon Islands Cuisine

The cuisine of the Solomon Islands is a reflection of its rich cultural heritage, diverse ecosystems, and the resourcefulness of its people. Situated in the tropical South Pacific, these islands offer a delectable array of flavors, drawing from the land and sea.

Seafood is the undisputed star of Solomon Islands cuisine. The pristine waters surrounding the archipelago teem with marine life, providing an abundant source of sustenance. Fish, in all its forms, takes center stage on the dinner table. Tuna, mahi-mahi, and snapper are among the favorites, prepared in myriad ways: grilled, fried, stewed, or wrapped in banana leaves and cooked in an earth oven known as a "lovo."

Coconut is a ubiquitous ingredient in Solomon Islands cuisine, used in various forms to add flavor and depth to dishes. Coconut milk, extracted from freshly grated coconut meat, is the base for many savory and sweet recipes. The famous "kokoda" is a beloved dish that features raw fish marinated in lime juice and mixed with coconut milk, fresh vegetables, and chili peppers, creating a refreshing and tangy flavor explosion.

Starchy staples like taro, yam, and sweet potatoes are dietary mainstays. These root crops are often roasted, boiled, or pounded into a starchy paste called "pulaka." Taro leaves are also used to make a delicious side dish known as "lap-lap," where they are layered with coconut milk and sometimes meat or fish, wrapped in banana leaves, and baked.

Sago, derived from the pith of certain palm trees, is another crucial source of carbohydrates in the Solomon Islands. It is processed into flour and used to make porridge or thickening agents for soups and stews. Sago dishes are often accompanied by coconut milk and seafood.

The Solomon Islands boast a rich tradition of culinary preservation methods. Fish, in particular, is sun-dried or smoked to extend its shelf life. Smoked fish, known as "bully beef," is a popular snack, enjoyed with fresh vegetables or starchy sides.

The islands' cuisine also features a variety of indigenous vegetables and fruits. Breadfruit, with its starchy, potato-like texture, is cooked in various ways, from roasting to frying, and is often served with coconut milk-based sauces. Pawpaw (papaya), bananas, and pineapples are just a few of the tropical fruits that add a burst of sweetness to Solomon Islands' dishes.

Local spices and flavorings such as turmeric, ginger, and chili peppers lend depth and complexity to the cuisine. The use of traditional herbs like "bush mint" and "taro leaves" adds unique flavor profiles to dishes.

Solomon Islands cuisine is not just about sustenance; it's a cultural expression. Meals are often shared communally, reinforcing the bonds of family and community. The process of food preparation and cooking is a time-honored tradition, passed down through generations, with each family having its own culinary secrets and recipes.

In recent years, the Solomon Islands has seen an emergence of culinary tourism, with chefs and food enthusiasts exploring the islands' unique ingredients and cooking techniques. This has led to a fusion of traditional and modern culinary influences, creating innovative dishes that celebrate the islands' heritage while embracing contemporary tastes.

As the world becomes more interconnected, Solomon Islands cuisine stands as a testament to the importance of preserving traditional foodways and culinary practices. It offers a mouthwatering journey into the heart of these vibrant and culturally rich islands, where food is not just sustenance but a celebration of life, community, and the bountiful offerings of land and sea.

Honiara - Capital City and Historical Hub

Honiara, the capital city of the Solomon Islands, is a bustling and vibrant urban center that stands as a testament to the nation's history, culture, and progress. Nestled on the northern coast of Guadalcanal Island, Honiara is not only the political and economic heart of the country but also a city rich in historical significance.

Honiara's roots can be traced back to World War II when it served as a strategic base for Allied forces in the Pacific. The city's development was greatly influenced by the conflict, and remnants of this era can still be found today. The iconic American War Memorial, located on Skyline Ridge, pays tribute to the U.S. Marines who fought in the Battle of Guadalcanal and is a prominent historical landmark.

The National Museum, located in Honiara, houses a remarkable collection of artifacts and exhibits that provide insights into the nation's cultural heritage and history. It is a must-visit destination for those seeking a deeper understanding of the Solomon Islands' diverse indigenous cultures and traditions.

Point Cruz, a picturesque area along Honiara's waterfront, was the site where John F. Kennedy served as a naval officer during World War II. The Kennedy Island, named in his honor, is located just off the coast and serves as a reminder of this connection.

Honiara's urban landscape reflects both its history and modernity. The city is a fusion of traditional and contemporary architecture, with government buildings, markets, shops, and residential areas coexisting harmoniously. The bustling Central Market is a hub of activity, offering an array of fresh produce, handicrafts, and local goods.

The city's waterfront area is a vibrant part of Honiara, with a bustling harbor and stunning views of the surrounding islands. The Central Wharf is a gathering place for locals and visitors alike, providing a glimpse into daily life in the Solomon Islands. It's also the departure point for boat trips to neighboring islands.

Honiara's diverse population includes people from various regions of the Solomon Islands, resulting in a rich tapestry of cultures and traditions. This cultural diversity is celebrated through music, dance, and festivals, with many events held in the city throughout the year.

As the capital city, Honiara is the political and administrative center of the Solomon Islands. The Parliament House, located in the city, is where the nation's legislative proceedings take place. The Prime Minister's Office, government ministries, and foreign embassies are also based in Honiara.

Honiara's infrastructure has steadily improved over the years, with paved roads, modern facilities, and amenities making it a more accessible and comfortable destination for residents and tourists alike. The city's medical facilities, educational institutions, and transportation networks continue to evolve, serving the needs of its growing population.

In recent years, Honiara has seen a surge in tourism, with visitors coming to explore its historical sites, vibrant markets, and natural beauty. The city serves as a gateway to the Solomon Islands' stunning landscapes, including pristine beaches, lush rainforests, and coral reefs teeming with marine life.

In conclusion, Honiara is not just a capital city; it's a living testament to the Solomon Islands' past, present, and future. Its history is intertwined with the global events of World War II, its culture is a vibrant reflection of indigenous traditions, and its development is a testament to the nation's progress. As the heart of the Solomon Islands, Honiara welcomes travelers with open arms, inviting them to explore its rich heritage and experience the warmth and hospitality of its people.

Gizo - Gateway to Western Province

Gizo, located in the Western Province of the Solomon Islands, is a tropical paradise that beckons travelers with its stunning natural beauty, rich cultural heritage, and opportunities for adventure. As the provincial capital and the second-largest town in the country, Gizo serves as the gateway to Western Province's diverse and captivating offerings.

Gizo's allure begins with its breathtaking surroundings. Situated on Ghizo Island, part of the larger New Georgia Group, the town is surrounded by crystal-clear waters, coral reefs, and lush green hills. The nearby islands, each with its unique charm, provide endless opportunities for exploration and relaxation.

The town itself is a charming blend of tradition and modernity. The market in the center of town is a bustling hub where locals sell fresh produce, seafood, handicrafts, and more. It's a vibrant place to experience the daily life of the Western Province's diverse communities.

Gizo is known for its connection to World War II history. Kennedy Island, just a short boat ride away, is where a young John F. Kennedy and his crew were shipwrecked during the war. The island is named in his honor and serves as a reminder of the historical significance of the area.

For history enthusiasts, the Gizo War Museum houses an impressive collection of artifacts, photographs, and exhibits related to World War II and the battles that took place in the Solomon Islands. It provides a fascinating glimpse into this pivotal period in history.

One of Gizo's main attractions is its proximity to some of the world's most pristine coral reefs. Diving and snorkeling enthusiasts flock to the Western Province to explore underwater wonders such as the famous "Kennedy Bomber" wreck, where a U.S. bomber plane rests on the ocean floor. The clear waters offer exceptional visibility and a dazzling array of marine life, including colorful coral formations, reef fish, sharks, and dolphins.

The picturesque Marovo Lagoon, the largest saltwater lagoon in the world, is a short boat ride from Gizo. It's a UNESCO World Heritage site, celebrated for its stunning beauty and rich cultural traditions. Visitors can explore traditional villages, witness intricate woodcarving demonstrations, and savor local cuisine.

Adventure seekers will find plenty of opportunities to satisfy their craving for excitement. Kayaking through mangrove forests, hiking to panoramic viewpoints, and embarking on boat trips to nearby islands are just a few of the activities available in the region. The island of Kolombangara, with its volcanic peaks and lush rainforests, offers challenging hiking adventures for the intrepid.

Gizo's culinary scene is a delightful fusion of traditional Solomon Islands dishes and international cuisine. Fresh seafood is a highlight, with dishes like coconut-crusted fish and seafood curries gracing menus. The town's eateries offer a welcoming atmosphere, allowing visitors to savor local flavors while enjoying stunning ocean views.

Accommodation options in Gizo cater to a range of preferences, from waterfront bungalows to cozy guesthouses. The warm hospitality of the locals ensures that visitors feel at home, making their stay in Gizo even more memorable.

In conclusion, Gizo is the epitome of tropical paradise, offering a harmonious blend of natural beauty, cultural richness, and adventure. As the gateway to Western Province, it invites travelers to immerse themselves in its history, dive into its pristine waters, and explore the diverse landscapes that make this corner of the Solomon Islands an unforgettable destination. Gizo is not just a place; it's an experience that captures the essence of the South Pacific's allure.

Tensions and Triumphs in Auki

Auki, the provincial capital of Malaita Province in the Solomon Islands, is a town that has witnessed its share of both tensions and triumphs throughout its history. Nestled on the northern coast of Malaita Island, Auki is not only a hub of commerce and administration but also a place where the complexities of culture, politics, and tradition have played out.

The town's history is intertwined with the broader context of the Solomon Islands' path to independence. During the colonial era, Auki, like many other parts of the archipelago, experienced the impact of European influence. The arrival of missionaries and colonial administrators brought significant changes to the way of life for the indigenous peoples of Malaita.

As the country moved toward self-governance and eventually independence in the latter half of the 20th century, Auki, like other provincial capitals, became a focal point for political and administrative activities. It played a pivotal role in the shaping of the nation's political landscape and governance structures.

However, Auki has not been without its challenges. The Solomon Islands experienced a period of ethnic tensions and conflict in the late 1990s, and Auki was not immune to the effects of this upheaval. The tensions had a profound impact on the town and its residents, disrupting daily life and causing hardship for many.

In the aftermath of the conflict, the people of Auki, along with the rest of the nation, embarked on a journey of reconciliation and rebuilding. The town became a symbol of resilience and determination as communities worked together to heal wounds, restore infrastructure, and rebuild trust.

One of the significant achievements during this period was the disarmament and demobilization of former combatants. This process paved the way for the reintegration of former fighters into their communities and the restoration of peace and stability.

In the years that followed, Auki and Malaita Province witnessed progress in various sectors, including education, healthcare, and infrastructure development. Schools were rebuilt, healthcare services were expanded, and efforts were made to strengthen the province's economic base.

The resilience and resourcefulness of the people of Auki have been evident in their efforts to revive traditional practices and preserve their cultural heritage. Malaita Province is known for its vibrant customs, including traditional dance, music, and art. These cultural expressions serve as a source of pride and identity for the residents of Auki.

Today, Auki continues to evolve and adapt to the changing dynamics of the Solomon Islands. It remains a center of administration and commerce for Malaita Province, with a growing population and a bustling marketplace. The town is connected to the broader region through its port and transportation networks, facilitating trade and movement between the islands.

Auki's journey reflects the broader story of the Solomon Islands, marked by a complex interplay of history, tradition, resilience, and progress. As the nation continues to move forward, Auki stands as a testament to the indomitable spirit of its people and their ability to overcome challenges and build a better future. It is a place where tensions have given way to triumphs, and where the past and present are intertwined in the ongoing narrative of the Solomon Islands.

Exploring the Lush Choiseul Island

Choiseul Island, situated in the Western Province of the Solomon Islands, is a lush and unspoiled paradise that beckons adventurers and nature enthusiasts with its breathtaking landscapes, vibrant culture, and rich biodiversity. As one of the largest islands in the archipelago, Choiseul Island offers a treasure trove of experiences for those willing to explore its verdant beauty.

The island's name, "Choiseul," is a nod to the French explorer Étienne François de Choiseul, who charted these waters in the 18th century. However, long before European contact, Choiseul Island was inhabited by indigenous peoples who have maintained their traditional way of life for centuries.

One of the island's defining features is its lush rainforests that cover much of its interior. Towering trees, dense vegetation, and meandering rivers create a pristine and enchanting environment. Choiseul's forests are home to an astonishing variety of flora and fauna, including numerous endemic species found nowhere else on Earth.

For nature enthusiasts, Choiseul Island offers a chance to immerse themselves in the wilderness. Hiking trails wind through the rainforest, leading to hidden waterfalls, tranquil streams, and panoramic viewpoints that offer sweeping vistas of the surrounding landscapes. The island's isolation and limited infrastructure have helped preserve its natural beauty, making it a haven for eco-tourism.

Choiseul Island is also renowned for its vibrant coral reefs and marine life. Snorkeling and diving enthusiasts are drawn to the crystalline waters that surround the island, where they can explore the kaleidoscope of colors beneath the surface. The reefs are teeming with an abundance of marine creatures, including colorful fish, sea turtles, and mesmerizing coral formations.

The indigenous cultures of Choiseul Island are rich and diverse. The island is home to several distinct ethnic groups, each with its unique traditions and languages. Visitors have the opportunity to engage with these communities, learn about their customs, and witness traditional dances, ceremonies, and rituals that have been passed down through generations.

One of the island's cultural highlights is the vibrant woodcarving tradition. Choiseul is renowned for its skilled artisans who create intricate carvings from local woods. These carvings often depict traditional stories, ancestral figures, and the natural world, and they serve as both artistic expressions and cultural artifacts.

The island's residents rely on subsistence agriculture and fishing for their livelihoods. Taro, yam, sweet potatoes, and sago are among the staple crops, while fishing in the surrounding waters provides a vital source of protein. Visitors can experience traditional fishing methods and enjoy freshly caught seafood prepared in local dishes.

Choiseul Island's remote location and limited tourist infrastructure mean that it remains off the beaten path for most travelers. However, for those seeking an authentic and unspoiled experience, this is a destination of unparalleled allure. The island's untouched landscapes, rich cultural heritage, and warm hospitality make it a hidden gem in the South Pacific.

In conclusion, exploring Choiseul Island is a journey into the heart of the Solomon Islands' natural beauty and cultural richness. Its lush rainforests, pristine reefs, and vibrant communities offer a glimpse into a world where tradition and nature are intertwined. As travelers venture into the depths of this captivating island, they discover a place where time seems to stand still, and the wonders of the natural world and the resilience of indigenous cultures are celebrated in harmony.

Ancient Mysteries of Malaita

Malaita, one of the largest islands in the Solomon Islands archipelago, holds within its dense jungles and remote landscapes a tapestry of ancient mysteries that continue to intrigue and captivate explorers, archaeologists, and historians. As visitors delve into the heart of this island, they are immersed in a world where the secrets of the past come to life.

The history of Malaita stretches back thousands of years, with evidence of human habitation dating back to the Lapita culture, one of the earliest seafaring societies in the Pacific. The Lapita people, known for their distinctive pottery, left their mark on the island, and their legacy is a source of fascination for researchers who seek to unravel the mysteries of their migration patterns and cultural practices.

One of the most enigmatic aspects of Malaita's history is the presence of ancient stone megaliths known as "Alofa'aga." These massive stone structures, resembling upright pillars or columns, are scattered across the island's interior. Their purpose and origin remain a subject of debate among scholars. Some suggest that they served as markers for ceremonial or navigational purposes, while others propose that they had spiritual significance.

The remote Fiu River, winding its way through the island's rainforest, is home to another puzzling relic of the past. Here, nestled among the trees, are ancient stone statues known as "talafar." These statues, carved from local stone, represent human figures with elongated bodies and distinctive facial features. The exact purpose and meaning behind these statues remain shrouded in mystery, as they defy easy interpretation.

The island's rich oral traditions and folklore add another layer of intrigue to Malaita's history. The stories passed down through generations often reference ancient practices, spirits, and mythical creatures that inhabited the island. These tales provide glimpses into the beliefs and worldviews of Malaita's indigenous peoples, who have maintained their cultural heritage despite the passage of time.

Malaita is also known for its intricate woodcarving traditions, which are deeply intertwined with its cultural history. The woodcarvings, with their intricate designs and symbolism, often depict ancestral figures and spiritual beings. They serve as a testament to the island's artistic heritage and the preservation of its cultural identity.

The island's rugged terrain, dense forests, and secluded valleys have made it challenging for researchers to uncover the full extent of its archaeological treasures. Expeditions into the interior have revealed ancient burial sites, pottery fragments, and tools that shed light on the daily lives of Malaita's early inhabitants.

As visitors venture into the heart of Malaita, they are welcomed by the warmth and hospitality of its communities. The island's residents, who have a deep connection to their ancestral lands, are eager to share their traditions and stories, offering a unique window into the island's ancient past.

In conclusion, the ancient mysteries of Malaita are a testament to the enduring allure of the Solomon Islands' cultural and archaeological heritage. The island's enigmatic stone structures, mysterious statues, and rich oral traditions continue to beckon those who seek to unravel the secrets of its past. As explorers delve into the heart of this remote and captivating island, they embark on a journey of discovery, where the echoes of history and the spirits of the ancients remain ever-present, waiting to be uncovered and celebrated.

The Serene Beauty of Santa Isabel

Santa Isabel, one of the larger islands in the Solomon Islands archipelago, is a place of breathtaking natural beauty and cultural richness that beckons travelers seeking serenity and adventure in equal measure. Nestled in the South Pacific, this island paradise offers a glimpse into a world where pristine landscapes and vibrant communities coexist harmoniously.

One of the island's most defining features is its lush rainforests that carpet much of its interior. Towering trees, dense undergrowth, and winding rivers create a pristine and enchanting environment. Santa Isabel's forests are not just a sight to behold but also a refuge for an incredible array of wildlife, including unique bird species such as the Santa Isabel monarch and the black-faced robin.

Santa Isabel's pristine rivers and waterways are a source of both beauty and utility for its communities. They provide essential transportation routes, connecting villages and towns across the island. Visitors can embark on boat journeys along these serene waterways, offering a unique perspective on the island's landscapes and providing opportunities for encounters with local residents.

The island's coastline is a captivating blend of white sandy beaches, palm-fringed shores, and vibrant coral reefs. The crystal-clear waters are teeming with marine life, making Santa Isabel a haven for snorkelers and divers. The marine biodiversity here is astounding, with colorful fish, rays, sharks, and an abundance of coral species.

Santa Isabel's indigenous cultures are rich and diverse. The island is home to several ethnic groups, each with its unique traditions and languages. Visitors have the opportunity to immerse themselves in these communities, experiencing their customs, enjoying traditional dances, and participating in cultural ceremonies that provide insight into the island's rich heritage.

The island's residents rely on subsistence agriculture and fishing for their livelihoods. Taro, yam, sweet potatoes, and sago are among the staple crops, while the bountiful seas provide an essential source of protein. Visitors can experience traditional farming practices and enjoy freshly caught seafood prepared in local dishes.

The indigenous peoples of Santa Isabel are known for their artistic talents, particularly in woodcarving. Local artisans craft intricate wooden sculptures, masks, and canoes, reflecting their deep connection to the natural world and their cultural heritage. These art forms serve as both artistic expressions and cultural artifacts.

Santa Isabel's communities are characterized by their warmth and hospitality, welcoming visitors with open arms. Staying in locally run accommodations or guesthouses provides an opportunity to engage with island residents, learn about their way of life, and create lasting memories of cultural exchange.

As visitors explore the island, they are often drawn to its numerous natural wonders, including waterfalls, caves, and picturesque viewpoints. These hidden gems are a testament to Santa Isabel's diverse landscapes and provide opportunities for hiking and adventure.

In conclusion, Santa Isabel is a sanctuary of serene beauty, where nature's wonders and cultural traditions intertwine. Its lush rainforests, pristine waters, and vibrant communities offer a haven for those seeking to escape the hustle and bustle of modern life. As travelers embark on a journey through the island's landscapes and engage with its indigenous cultures, they discover a place where time seems to slow down, and the beauty of the natural world and the warmth of its people come together in perfect harmony. Santa Isabel is not just an island; it's an invitation to explore the serene and soul-enriching beauty of the South Pacific.

The Magical Marovo Lagoon

The Marovo Lagoon, nestled in the Western Province of the Solomon Islands, is a place of unparalleled natural beauty and mystique. Widely regarded as one of the world's most magnificent saltwater lagoons, Marovo beckons travelers to immerse themselves in its magical embrace and discover the secrets hidden within its pristine waters and lush surroundings.

This remarkable lagoon stretches over 700 square kilometers, making it the largest saltwater lagoon in the world. Surrounded by a necklace of lush, densely forested islands, it is a haven for both nature enthusiasts and those seeking tranquility in an untouched paradise.

The name "Marovo" itself conjures images of enchantment and wonder, and rightly so. The lagoon's waters are a stunning tapestry of blues and greens, shimmering in the dappled sunlight that filters through the canopies of the surrounding rainforests. As one glides across its surface, the feeling of serenity and awe is palpable.

For those who venture beneath the lagoon's surface, a world of astonishing biodiversity unfolds. Marovo's coral reefs are nothing short of spectacular, boasting an incredible array of hard and soft corals, sea fans, and sponges. These vibrant ecosystems provide a refuge for countless marine species, from colorful reef fish to graceful sea turtles.

One of the most cherished treasures of Marovo is the dugong, a gentle marine mammal that has found sanctuary in the lagoon's seagrass beds. Dugongs are known for their elusive nature, and encountering one of these graceful creatures in the wild is a dream come true for many visitors.

The lagoon's abundant marine life extends to its diverse fish population. Snorkelers and divers are treated to a mesmerizing underwater world teeming with tropical fish species. Among the highlights are the giant clams that inhabit the lagoon's seabed, their vibrant colors adding to the kaleidoscope of marine beauty.

Marovo Lagoon is also steeped in cultural significance. The islands that encircle the lagoon are inhabited by indigenous communities that have called this place home for generations. The people of Marovo are known for their vibrant cultural traditions, including intricate woodcarving, vibrant dances, and traditional ceremonies that celebrate their connection to the land and sea.

Visitors to Marovo have the privilege of engaging with these communities, witnessing their artistic talents, and experiencing the warmth of their hospitality. The islanders are eager to share their stories and customs, providing insights into the rich cultural tapestry of the Solomon Islands.

Exploring the lagoon and its surrounding islands is an adventure in itself. Kayaking through the tranquil waters, visiting remote villages, and hiking to viewpoints that offer breathtaking panoramas of the lagoon are just a few of the experiences that await.

Accommodations in Marovo range from rustic eco-lodges to comfortable bungalows perched over the water, allowing guests to fall asleep to the soothing lullaby of gentle waves. These accommodations are designed to blend seamlessly with the natural environment, providing an immersive and eco-friendly experience.

In conclusion, the Marovo Lagoon is a place of magic and wonder, where the natural world and human culture intertwine in perfect harmony. Its pristine waters, vibrant coral reefs, and lush rainforests create an enchanting backdrop for unforgettable adventures and cultural encounters. As travelers explore the lagoon's mysteries and engage with its indigenous communities, they discover a place where the boundaries between reality and fantasy blur, leaving an indelible mark on the soul. Marovo is not just a destination; it's a journey into the heart of nature's magic, where every moment is an opportunity to be enchanted by the beauty of the South Pacific.

Rennell and Bellona: World Heritage Wonders

Rennell and Bellona, two remote islands in the Solomon Islands archipelago, stand as jewels in the crown of the South Pacific. These islands, although lesser-known compared to some of their neighbors, boast a unique and remarkable natural heritage that has earned them recognition as a UNESCO World Heritage Site.

Rennell and Bellona, together forming one province, are characterized by their isolation and pristine beauty. Rennell, the southernmost island, is the largest raised coral atoll in the world, and Bellona, its northern neighbor, is a raised limestone atoll. These geological formations alone set them apart as exceptional places of ecological significance.

The islands' claim to fame, however, extends below the surface of the water. The surrounding waters of Rennell and Bellona are home to some of the world's most extensive and biodiverse coral reefs. These reefs support a rich variety of marine life, including colorful corals, tropical fish, sharks, and sea turtles. The health and vibrancy of these reefs are a testament to the conservation efforts in place to protect this precious marine ecosystem.

One of the most extraordinary features of Rennell and Bellona is the massive Lake Tegano, found on Rennell Island. This pristine, freshwater lake occupies a significant portion of the island's interior and is an exceptional example of a naturally occurring lake within a raised coral atoll. Lake Tegano is not only ecologically significant but also culturally important to the local communities who rely on it for their livelihoods.

Rennell and Bellona are home to unique and endemic species, both on land and in the water. Birdwatchers are drawn to the islands by the chance to spot the Rennell fantail, a bird found only on Rennell Island, as well as other endemic species like the Rennell white-eye and the Bellona white-eye.

The islands are also rich in archaeological heritage, with evidence of early human habitation dating back over 700 years. Ancient settlements, stone tools, and other artifacts have been discovered, shedding light on the history and culture of the indigenous peoples who have called these islands home for centuries.

The cultural traditions of Rennell and Bellona are deeply rooted in the land and sea. The islanders have a strong connection to their natural environment, and their customs and rituals reflect this deep relationship. Traditional dances, songs, and ceremonies celebrate their heritage and the bounty of the ocean.

Visitors to Rennell and Bellona have the opportunity to engage with the local communities, experiencing their hospitality and learning about their way of life. The islanders are proud of their cultural traditions and are eager to share them with those who venture to these remote shores.

Accommodations on Rennell and Bellona range from guesthouses to eco-lodges, offering visitors a chance to stay close to nature while enjoying the comforts of modern amenities. The laid-back pace of life on the islands allows travelers to unwind, disconnect, and immerse themselves in the natural and cultural wonders of this UNESCO World Heritage Site.

In conclusion, Rennell and Bellona are hidden gems in the South Pacific, where natural beauty, ecological significance, and cultural richness converge. These islands offer a unique opportunity to explore a pristine marine environment, witness endemic species, and engage with indigenous communities that have preserved their traditions for generations. Rennell and Bellona stand as a testament to the remarkable biodiversity and cultural heritage of the Solomon Islands, inviting travelers to embark on a journey of discovery in a World Heritage wonderland.

Tikopia - The Island of Sustainability

Tikopia, a tiny island in the Solomon Islands archipelago, has earned global recognition as a remarkable model of sustainability and self-sufficiency. Situated in the South Pacific, this isolated paradise has captured the imagination of scholars, environmentalists, and travelers alike, showcasing the extraordinary ways in which a small community can thrive in harmony with its natural surroundings.

The island of Tikopia covers an area of just 5 square kilometers, making it one of the smallest inhabited islands in the Solomon Islands. Its remote location, far from the bustling urban centers of the modern world, has allowed its indigenous inhabitants to preserve their traditional way of life and maintain a unique and sustainable ecosystem.

One of the most striking aspects of Tikopia's sustainability is its agricultural practices. The islanders practice what is known as "integrated agroforestry," a system that combines the cultivation of crops, such as taro, yams, bananas, and sweet potatoes, with the careful management of forests. The dense forests provide valuable resources, including timber, wild foods, and materials for construction, while also acting as a buffer against soil erosion and extreme weather events.

Tikopia's agricultural system is a model of self-sufficiency. The islanders have developed intricate knowledge of their local environment, allowing them to sustainably manage their limited resources. The cultivation of root crops and tree crops is complemented by a reliance on fishing as a vital source of protein. Tikopians have mastered the art of fishing, using traditional methods such as fish traps and handlines to harvest the abundant marine life that surrounds their island.

The island's isolation has also contributed to its sustainability. Tikopia's limited contact with the outside world has helped preserve its traditional customs, including social hierarchies and cultural practices. These customs are deeply entwined with their sustainable way of life, reinforcing the importance of environmental stewardship and community cooperation.

The Tikopian concept of "utu" is central to their sustainability. Utu embodies the idea of reciprocal exchange and cooperation within the community. It fosters a sense of collective responsibility for the island's resources and ensures that everyone has access to the benefits of sustainable living.

Another remarkable aspect of Tikopia's sustainability is its population control measures. To prevent overpopulation and resource depletion, Tikopians practice a form of birth control known as "malo." This cultural practice, which restricts the number of children a couple can have, helps maintain a balance between the island's resources and its population.

Tikopia's sustainable way of life has attracted the attention of researchers and conservationists from around the world. They come to study the island's ecological and social systems, seeking insights that could inform more sustainable practices elsewhere.

The island's commitment to sustainability has also led to its inclusion in the UNESCO World Heritage List, recognizing its unique cultural and environmental significance. Tikopia stands as a living testament to the power of traditional knowledge and sustainable practices in the face of modern environmental challenges.

In conclusion, Tikopia is a shining example of how sustainability and self-sufficiency can coexist in harmony with the natural world. This tiny island, with its resilient community and time-tested practices, offers valuable lessons for a world grappling with issues of resource depletion and environmental degradation. Tikopia is not just an island; it's an inspiration and a beacon of hope for a more sustainable future.

Diving into the Deep: Solomon Islands' Reefs

The Solomon Islands, nestled in the heart of the South Pacific, are renowned worldwide for their extraordinary coral reefs. Beneath the crystal-clear waters of this tropical paradise lies an underwater wonderland that has captivated divers and marine enthusiasts for decades. Let's dive deep into the mesmerizing world of the Solomon Islands' reefs.

The Solomon Islands are part of the Coral Triangle, an area recognized as the global center of marine biodiversity. This geographic blessing has endowed the country with an astonishing variety of marine life and some of the most pristine coral reefs on the planet. It's no surprise that the Solomon Islands have become a mecca for divers seeking unparalleled underwater experiences.

One of the most remarkable features of the Solomon Islands' reefs is their diversity. The reefs here are home to a staggering array of corals, including hard corals, soft corals, and everything in between. These corals come in a kaleidoscope of colors and shapes, creating a mesmerizing underwater tapestry.

Divers and snorkelers are treated to an aquatic menagerie that includes vibrant reef fish, graceful sea turtles, and playful dolphins. The Solomon Islands' reefs also attract larger marine species, such as sharks and rays, adding an element of thrill to any dive adventure.

One of the country's most famous dive sites is the "Florida Islands," known for its dramatic drop-offs, swim-throughs, and a rich concentration of marine life. Here, divers can encounter schools of barracuda, colorful nudibranchs, and even the elusive hammerhead shark. The wrecks of World War II-era ships and aircraft also add an eerie, historical dimension to these underwater explorations.

The Solomon Islands offer diverse diving experiences, catering to both novice and experienced divers. For beginners, calm lagoons and shallow reefs provide a safe and gentle introduction to the world of underwater exploration. Advanced divers, on the other hand, can explore dramatic walls, deep channels, and underwater caves that plunge into the abyss.

One of the most unique and sought-after experiences in the Solomon Islands is "muck diving." This specialized form of diving involves exploring the sandy seabed for hidden treasures. Here, divers can discover bizarre and fascinating critters like the flamboyant cuttlefish, ghost pipefish, and various species of seahorses.

The Solomon Islands also offer the opportunity to witness natural phenomena that are nothing short of spectacular. One such phenomenon is the annual coral spawning, where corals release their eggs and sperm into the water in a synchronized dance of reproduction. This mesmerizing event draws scientists and enthusiasts alike to witness the underwater spectacle.

Conservation efforts in the Solomon Islands are crucial to preserving this marine paradise. Local communities, with the support of international organizations, are actively engaged in protecting their reefs and marine resources.

Marine sanctuaries and protected areas have been established to safeguard vulnerable ecosystems.

In conclusion, the Solomon Islands' reefs are a testament to the extraordinary beauty and biodiversity that lies beneath the waves of this tropical paradise. Whether you're an avid diver or simply a lover of the natural world, the underwater wonders of the Solomon Islands offer a glimpse into a realm of vibrant colors, incredible creatures, and awe-inspiring landscapes. It's a world that continues to inspire and educate, reminding us of the importance of conservation and the fragile beauty of our oceans. Dive in, explore, and be enchanted by the Solomon Islands' reefs, a true underwater Eden.

Birdwatching Paradise: Avian Wonders

The Solomon Islands, a remote archipelago in the South Pacific, are a hidden treasure for bird enthusiasts and ornithologists alike. With their lush rainforests, diverse ecosystems, and isolation from the mainland, these islands have become a haven for avian species found nowhere else on Earth. Let's embark on a journey through the avian wonders of the Solomon Islands.

The islands' tropical rainforests provide a rich and varied habitat for a stunning array of birdlife. One of the most iconic and sought-after species in the Solomon Islands is the Solomon Sea Eagle, a majestic bird of prey known for its distinctive white head and dark body. These impressive eagles can often be spotted soaring gracefully over the coastal regions.

Endemic species are the true gems of the Solomon Islands' avian world. Among these treasures is the Solomon Islands Kestrel, a small, strikingly colored bird that graces the forests with its presence. The Roviana Rail, another endemic species, can be found in the dense undergrowth, where it forages for insects and small invertebrates.

Birdwatchers are also drawn to the Solomon Islands to catch a glimpse of the elusive Solomon Islands Frogmouth, a master of camouflage that perfectly blends into the forest canopy. The critically endangered Heinrich's Nightjar is another rare find, its haunting calls echoing through the night in select parts of the islands.

The diversity of birdlife extends beyond the forests to the coastal and marine environments. Coastal areas are home to waders, shorebirds, and waterfowl, making them excellent birdwatching locations. The Solomon Islands provide critical habitat for migratory species that travel thousands of kilometers to find refuge and food along their migratory routes.

One of the remarkable features of birdwatching in the Solomon Islands is the opportunity to observe birds in their natural habitat without the crowds often associated with other birdwatching destinations. The islands' remote and pristine landscapes offer a sense of solitude and a chance to connect with nature in a profound way.

The traditional knowledge of the indigenous peoples of the Solomon Islands has played a significant role in bird conservation. Local communities have a deep understanding of their natural environment and have implemented conservation measures to protect their avian neighbors. These efforts include the establishment of community-managed conservation areas and the protection of critical nesting sites.

Visitors to the Solomon Islands can immerse themselves in birdwatching adventures guided by local experts who possess an intimate knowledge of the best locations and times to spot various species. Guided tours offer the chance to observe birds in their natural behaviors, such as feeding, nesting, and courtship displays.

The avian wonders of the Solomon Islands are not limited to the forests and coastlines. Offshore islands and islets provide additional opportunities to encounter seabirds like the Red-footed Booby, Brown Noddy, and the graceful

Frigatebird. These islands also serve as important breeding grounds for these seabird species.

In conclusion, the Solomon Islands are a birdwatching paradise, where the magic of avian diversity unfolds in lush rainforests, coastal habitats, and remote islets. With a rich tapestry of endemic and migratory species, these islands offer an unforgettable experience for bird enthusiasts and nature lovers. As visitors explore the Solomon Islands' avian wonders, they not only witness the beauty of these unique birds but also contribute to the conservation efforts that protect these treasures for generations to come. It's a world where the song of a bird can be a melody of hope, a reminder of the importance of preserving the natural wonders of our planet.

The Solomon Islands' Unique Marine Life

The Solomon Islands, cradled in the heart of the Pacific Ocean, boast a marine paradise unlike any other on Earth. These pristine waters, teeming with an extraordinary diversity of marine life, have earned the Solomon Islands a reputation as one of the world's premier dive destinations. Let's dive deep into the unique marine ecosystems that make these islands a treasure trove of biodiversity.

One of the defining features of the Solomon Islands' marine life is its incredible coral diversity. The reefs here are a testament to the vitality of the underwater world, hosting a dazzling variety of corals, including hard corals, soft corals, and black corals. These corals form the building blocks of the reef ecosystem, providing shelter and sustenance for countless species.

The sheer abundance and diversity of fish species in the Solomon Islands are staggering. From colorful reef fish like butterflyfish, angelfish, and parrotfish to pelagic giants like tuna and barracuda, the waters here are a vibrant symphony of colors and shapes. Divers can witness the breathtaking spectacle of schools of fish swirling in perfect unison, a testament to the intricate harmony of marine life.

One of the most coveted encounters for divers in the Solomon Islands is the opportunity to swim with graceful sea turtles. Several species, including the green sea turtle and the hawksbill sea turtle, call these waters home. These gentle creatures glide through the clear blue waters, a reminder of the importance of conservation efforts to protect their nesting sites.

Sharks are also a common sight in the Solomon Islands, and divers can encounter a variety of species, including reef sharks, hammerhead sharks, and the awe-inspiring whale sharks. These apex predators play a vital role in maintaining the health and balance of the marine ecosystem.

The Solomon Islands' marine biodiversity extends beyond the reefs to its spectacular pelagic encounters. The islands are renowned for their incredible opportunities to witness large marine life, such as manta rays and dolphins, as they glide through the open ocean. These encounters are a testament to the importance of preserving the open seas that surround the archipelago.

For macro enthusiasts, the Solomon Islands offer the thrill of discovering tiny and cryptic creatures that hide among the coral and seafloor. Critters like pygmy seahorses, ghost pipefish, and colorful nudibranchs are a delight for those with a keen eye and a macro lens.

In addition to its vibrant coral reefs and diverse fish populations, the Solomon Islands are also home to rare and elusive species. The islands are a crucial nesting site for the critically endangered hawksbill turtle, and they provide important breeding grounds for migratory species like the sooty tern.

Conservation efforts in the Solomon Islands are vital to protecting its unique marine life. Local communities, in collaboration with government agencies and international organizations, have established marine protected areas and sustainable fishing practices to safeguard the health of the reefs and the livelihoods of those who depend on them.

In conclusion, the Solomon Islands' marine life is a testament to the wonders of the underwater world. From the vibrant reefs to the open ocean, this archipelago is a showcase of marine biodiversity that continues to inspire divers, researchers, and conservationists. As visitors explore the unique marine ecosystems of the Solomon Islands, they bear witness to the beauty and fragility of our oceans, a reminder of the urgent need to protect these precious underwater treasures for future generations.

Preserving the Past: Museums and Heritage Sites

The Solomon Islands, a land of natural beauty and cultural richness, hold a treasure trove of history and heritage waiting to be uncovered. The preservation of this legacy is paramount, and the islands are home to a network of museums and heritage sites that serve as custodians of the past.

In Honiara, the capital city, the National Museum and Cultural Centre stands as a repository of the nation's history and culture. Here, visitors can explore a vast collection of artifacts, including traditional tools, ceremonial masks, and intricately crafted canoes. The museum's exhibits offer a window into the diverse traditions and customs of the Solomon Islands' various indigenous communities.

The Vilu War Museum, also in Honiara, pays homage to the significant role the islands played during World War II. This open-air museum houses a remarkable collection of war relics, from aircraft wrecks to artillery pieces. It serves as a poignant reminder of the islands' wartime history and the sacrifices made by both Allied and Japanese forces.

Tucked away in the heart of the islands is the Tenaru Falls Historical Site, a place of great significance in the annals of World War II. It was here, in 1942, that the First Battle of the Matanikau took place, a fierce confrontation between American and Japanese forces. Today, visitors can explore the jungle trail to the falls, where remnants of the battle still lie hidden in the undergrowth.

In the Western Province, Gizo is home to the Peter Joseph World War II Museum, dedicated to preserving the history of the war in the Solomon Islands. The museum's exhibits include personal artifacts, photographs, and documents that provide insights into the experiences of soldiers and civilians during this tumultuous period.

Auki, the provincial capital of Malaita, houses the Langa Langa Lagoon Cultural Village, where visitors can immerse themselves in the traditions and customs of the local Malaitan people. This living museum offers a glimpse into daily life, showcasing traditional dance, music, and crafts.

The Marovo Lagoon, a UNESCO World Heritage site, is not only a natural wonder but also a repository of cultural heritage. Here, the Marovo Lagoon Cultural Festival allows visitors to witness traditional ceremonies, canoe races, and craftsmanship demonstrations, providing a unique opportunity to engage with local culture.

Throughout the islands, various heritage sites commemorate the islands' rich past. From ancient petroglyphs etched into the rocks to sacred shrines and burial sites, these places offer a glimpse into the spiritual and historical dimensions of the Solomon Islands.

The preservation of the Solomon Islands' heritage goes beyond museums and sites; it is a collective effort involving local communities, governments, and international organizations. Cultural festivals, workshops, and educational programs are integral to passing down traditional knowledge and skills to future generations.

The Solomon Islands' heritage sites and museums not only preserve the past but also provide a platform for cultural exchange and understanding. Visitors have the opportunity to connect with the islands' rich tapestry of cultures and gain a deeper appreciation for the traditions that have shaped these lands.

In conclusion, the Solomon Islands' commitment to preserving its past is evident in the museums, heritage sites, and cultural festivals that celebrate its history and traditions. These institutions serve as guardians of the islands' cultural legacy, ensuring that the stories of the past continue to inspire and educate. As visitors explore these sites and engage with local communities, they become part of the ongoing narrative of the Solomon Islands, where the past is cherished, and the future is built upon the foundations of history and heritage.

Cultural Festivals and Celebrations

The Solomon Islands are not just a place of stunning natural beauty and historical significance; they are also a vibrant tapestry of cultures and traditions. Throughout the year, these islands come alive with a colorful array of cultural festivals and celebrations that offer a window into the rich and diverse heritage of the people who call this archipelago home.

One of the most eagerly anticipated cultural events in the Solomon Islands is the "Solomon Islands Festival of Arts" or "Fest'Napuan." This festival, held annually in Port Vila, Vanuatu, brings together artists, musicians, dancers, and performers from across the Pacific region. It is a celebration of cultural exchange and creativity, where attendees can witness traditional dances, listen to traditional music, and view exquisite handicrafts.

In Honiara, the capital city, the "Solomon Islands National Arts Council Festival" is a showcase of local talent. Artists and performers from various provinces gather to display their skills in music, dance, and visual arts. It's an opportunity for communities to share their unique cultural expressions and for visitors to immerse themselves in the vibrant atmosphere.

The Malaita Festival, held in Auki, is a celebration of Malaitan culture and traditions. It features traditional dances, canoe races, and displays of traditional crafts. It's a moment for Malaitans to come together and reaffirm their cultural identity, and for outsiders to witness the richness of this province's heritage.

The "Langa Langa Festival" is another significant cultural event in Malaita, centered around the Langa Langa Lagoon. It showcases the unique music, dance, and traditions of the local people. Visitors can enjoy performances by traditional string bands, witness the creation of intricate shell money, and experience the warm hospitality of the Langa Langa community.

Throughout the year, different provinces host their own festivals, each offering a unique glimpse into the local culture. The Western Province's "Festival of the Arts" is a vibrant celebration of Melanesian traditions, featuring captivating performances and displays of traditional crafts. The "Choiseul Cultural Festival" highlights the distinct culture of Choiseul Province, while the "Temotu Provincial Day" allows the people of Temotu to share their heritage with the world.

In Rennell and Bellona Province, the "Lake Tegano World Heritage Site Festival" celebrates the natural and cultural wonders of this World Heritage-listed site. Visitors can explore the pristine lake, witness traditional dances, and learn about the unique way of life of the local communities.

These festivals are not just showcases of culture but also opportunities for cultural exchange. They provide a platform for communities from different provinces to come together, share their traditions, and learn from one another. Visitors are often welcomed with open arms, invited to participate in dances, and encouraged to try their hand at traditional crafts.

Traditional foods are an integral part of these festivals, offering a delicious journey into the culinary traditions of the Solomon Islands. Dishes like "kokoda" (a ceviche-like dish with fish marinated in coconut milk and lime), "lamb flap" (grilled lamb with coconut), and "tarosi" (fermented fish paste) are just a few of the culinary delights to savor.

In conclusion, the cultural festivals and celebrations of the Solomon Islands are windows into a world of diverse traditions, vibrant arts, and warm hospitality. They not only celebrate the past but also bridge the gap between generations and connect the islands' people with the global community. These festivals are a testament to the resilience of culture and the importance of preserving and sharing the rich heritage of the Solomon Islands with the world. As visitors partake in these celebrations, they become part of the ongoing story of these islands, where culture thrives and traditions endure.

Tourism and Sustainable Travel in the Solomon Islands

Tourism in the Solomon Islands is a journey into the heart of the South Pacific, where travelers discover a world of natural wonders, cultural richness, and warm hospitality. As this remote archipelago gains recognition as a travel destination, the importance of sustainable tourism practices becomes increasingly evident. Let's delve into the realm of tourism and sustainable travel in the Solomon Islands.

The Solomon Islands, with their pristine coral reefs, lush rainforests, and vibrant cultures, offer a unique and authentic travel experience. While still relatively off the beaten path compared to other tropical destinations, the islands have seen a steady growth in tourism in recent years. Visitors are drawn to the opportunity to explore untouched landscapes, immerse themselves in local culture, and partake in eco-adventures.

Sustainable travel practices are at the forefront of the Solomon Islands' tourism industry. Local communities and government authorities recognize the need to protect their natural environment and cultural heritage while ensuring that tourism benefits local economies. Efforts have been made to strike a balance between the desire for increased tourism and the preservation of what makes the islands special.

Eco-tourism initiatives play a crucial role in sustainable travel in the Solomon Islands. The islands' lush rainforests, clear waters, and diverse marine life offer a wealth of opportunities for eco-conscious travelers. Visitors can explore pristine hiking trails, embark on birdwatching excursions, and dive into vibrant coral gardens while adhering to responsible and low-impact practices.

Community-based tourism projects are another cornerstone of sustainable travel in the Solomon Islands. Many communities have opened their doors to visitors, offering homestays, guided tours, and cultural experiences. These initiatives allow travelers to directly support local livelihoods while gaining insight into traditional ways of life.

Resorts and accommodations in the Solomon Islands increasingly prioritize sustainability. Eco-friendly resorts utilize renewable energy sources, implement waste reduction measures, and support local conservation efforts. Many resorts are committed to responsible fishing practices and minimize their environmental footprint.

Marine conservation is a focal point of sustainable travel in the Solomon Islands. The preservation of the coral reefs, which are among the world's most diverse and healthy, is of paramount importance. Initiatives like the "Hapi Isles Program" and "Save Our Seas" work to protect the marine environment, raise awareness about responsible diving and snorkeling practices, and promote sustainable seafood choices.

The Solomon Islands also strive to minimize the carbon footprint of travel to and within the archipelago. Efforts are being made to improve transportation options and reduce reliance on fossil fuels. Sustainable transportation initiatives include the use of solar-powered boats and the promotion of electric vehicles.

Sustainable travel goes hand in hand with cultural sensitivity and respect. Visitors are encouraged to engage with local communities in a meaningful way, respecting traditional customs and seeking permission before entering sacred sites. Learning about and appreciating local cultures are integral to the travel experience in the Solomon Islands.

In conclusion, tourism in the Solomon Islands holds the promise of sustainable growth, where travelers can connect with nature and culture while contributing to the well-being of local communities. Sustainable travel practices are not merely a trend but a commitment to safeguarding the islands' natural and cultural treasures for generations to come. As visitors explore the Solomon Islands with a sense of responsibility and respect, they become stewards of this pristine paradise, ensuring that its allure endures for years to come.

Conclusion

In the heart of the Pacific Ocean lies an archipelago of captivating beauty and rich history—the Solomon Islands. This book has been a journey through time, delving into the fascinating tapestry of the Solomon Islands' past and present. From the emergence of these islands from the depths of the ocean to their vibrant cultural traditions, from tribal conflicts to the tumultuous period of European exploration, from the crucible of World War II to the triumphant path to independence, we have explored the many facets of this extraordinary nation.

The Solomon Islands have always been a place of mystery and wonder. The early indigenous inhabitants, with their intricate cultures and spiritual beliefs, laid the foundation for the unique diversity that characterizes these islands today. Navigators from the distant Polynesian islands connected these remote shores, leaving their indelible mark on the culture and traditions of the region.

Warriors of the islands engaged in tribal conflicts that shaped the course of history, while the arrival of European explorers opened new chapters in the islands' story. Spanish and Portuguese encounters, though brief, left a lasting impact, and the British and German colonial era transformed the islands' social and political landscape.

World War II brought the Solomon Islands to the forefront of global history, with the Battle of Guadalcanal standing as a testament to the courage and sacrifice of those who fought on these shores. The post-war struggles for independence signaled a new era, as the islands navigated their path to self-governance.

With sovereignty achieved, the Solomon Islands faced modern challenges and political developments, seeking stability and progress while preserving their cultural heritage. The islands' vibrant arts, crafts, music, dance, and healing traditions continue to thrive, providing a unique window into the lives of the people who call this place home.

The Solomon Islands' natural world is equally captivating. Its flora and fauna, from lush rainforests to diverse marine life, make it a biodiversity hotspot. Birdwatching enthusiasts, divers, and nature lovers find solace in the islands' breathtaking landscapes and unique wildlife.

As we embarked on this literary journey, we also savored the flavors of Solomon Islands cuisine—a gastronomic journey of discovery, from coconut-infused dishes to exotic tropical fruits.

Throughout this narrative, we explored the historic cities and provinces, each with its own distinct character and significance. Honiara, the bustling capital and historical hub; Gizo, the gateway to Western Province; Auki, a place of tensions and triumphs; Choiseul Island, a lush paradise waiting to be explored; Malaita, with its ancient mysteries; Santa Isabel, a serene beauty; Marovo Lagoon, a magical wonder; Rennell and Bellona, World Heritage wonders; Tikopia, the island of sustainability; and countless other destinations that make the Solomon Islands a place of endless exploration.

As we conclude this journey through the Solomon Islands, we are reminded of the enduring allure of this archipelago—a place where nature and culture, history and modernity, coexist in harmony. The Solomon Islands invite travelers to step into a world of beauty, intrigue, and warmth, where every visit is a chance to contribute to the preservation of this unique paradise.

In closing, the story of the Solomon Islands is an ongoing narrative, one that continues to be written by the people who call these islands home and by those who are fortunate enough to experience their wonders. As travelers, scholars, and admirers of this remarkable nation, we are all stewards of its past and guardians of its future. May the Solomon Islands' legacy of beauty, culture, and resilience endure for generations to come, inviting new generations to discover and cherish its treasures.

Thank you for taking the time to read this book about the fascinating history, culture, and natural wonders of the Solomon Islands. I hope you found this journey through its pages as enlightening and captivating as I did while writing it.

If you enjoyed the book and found it informative, I kindly ask for your support by leaving a positive review. Your feedback is invaluable and can help others discover the beauty and richness of the Solomon Islands through these words.

Your review will not only encourage other readers to explore this remarkable nation but also inspire me to continue sharing stories and knowledge about the world's diverse and captivating places.

Once again, thank you for your time and for being part of this literary adventure. Your support is greatly appreciated!

Printed in Great Britain
by Amazon